Build-a-Skill Instant Books

Beginning and Ending Consonant Sounds

Written by
Vicky Shiotsu

Editor: Stacey Faulkner
Illustrator: Darcy Tom
Cover Illustrator: Rick Grayson
Designer: The Development Source
Art Director: Moonhee Pak
Project Director: Betsy Morris

© 2015 Creative Teaching Press Inc., Huntington Beach, CA 92649
Reproduction of activities in any manner for use in the classroom and not for commercial sale is permissible.
Reproduction of these materials for an entire school or for a school system is strictly prohibited.

Printed in China through Colorcraft Ltd., Hong Kong

Table of Contents

Introduction 2

Making and Using the Instant Books 3

Instant Books

Beginning Sounds: *b, c, d* 5

Beginning Sounds Picture Cards: *b, c, d* 6

Beginning Sounds: *f, g, h* 7

Beginning Sounds Picture Cards: *f, g, h* 8

My Animal Book

   (beginning consonants *b–h*) 9

Beginning Sounds: *j, k, l* 10

Beginning Sounds Picture Cards: *j, k, l* 11

Beginning Sounds: *m, n, p* 12

Beginning Sounds Picture Cards: *m, n, p* 13

My Playtime Book

   (beginning consonants *j–p*) 14

Beginning Sounds: *q, r, s* 15

Beginning Sounds Picture Cards: *q, r, s* 16

Beginning Sounds: *t, v, w* 17

Beginning Sounds Picture Cards: *t, v, w* 18

Beginning Sounds: *w, y, z* 19

Beginning Sounds Picture Cards: *w, y, z* 20

Things at Home

   (beginning consonants *r–z*) 21

Ending Sounds Word Wallet: *b, d, f* 22

Ending Sounds Wallet Pictures: *b, d, f* 23

Ending Sounds Word Wallet: *g, k, l* 24

Ending Sounds Wallet Pictures: *g, k, l* 25

Ending Sounds Word Wallet: *m, n, s* 26

Ending Sounds Wallet Pictures: *m, n, s* 27

Ending Sounds Word Wallet: *p, t, x* 28

Ending Sounds Wallet Pictures: *p, t, x* 29

Trucking Along

   (beginning and ending consonants) 30

Now Hear This!

   (beginning and ending consonants) 31

I Know Letters and Sounds!

   (beginning and ending consonants) 32

Introduction

About the Build-a-Skill Instant Books Series

The *Build-a-Skill Instant Books* series features a variety of reproducible instant books that focus on important reading and math skills covered in the primary classroom. Each instant book is easy to make, and once children become familiar with the basic formats that appear throughout the series, they will be able to make new books with little help. Children will love the unique, manipulative quality of the books and will want to read them over and over again as they gain mastery of basic learning skills!

About the Build-a-Skill Instant Books: Beginning and Ending Consonant Sounds

This book features beginning and ending consonants in fun and easy-to-make instant books. Children will develop fine motor skills and practice following directions as they cut, fold, and staple the reproducible pages together to make flip books, strip books, shape books, and word wallets. As children read and reread their instant books, they will increase their ability to recognize the relationship between letters and sounds, and strengthen their decoding skills.

Refer to the Table of Contents to help with lesson planning. Choose instant book activities that fit with the curriculum goals in your regular or ELL classroom. Use the instant books to practice skills or introduce new ones. Directions for making the instant books appear on pages 3 and 4. These should be copied and sent along with the book patterns when assigning a bookmaking activity as homework.

Making and Using the Instant Books

All of the instant books in this resource require only one or two pieces of paper. Copy the pages on white copy paper or card stock, or use colored paper to jazz up and vary the formats. Children will love personalizing their instant books by coloring them, adding construction paper covers, or decorating them with collage materials such as wiggly eyes, ribbon, and stickers. Customize the instant books by making additional picture cards that reflect students' interests or that reinforce vocabulary from content areas such as social studies and science.

Children can make instant books as an enrichment activity when their regular classwork is done, as a learning center activity during guided reading time, or as a homework assignment. They can place completed instant books in their classroom book boxes and then read and reread the books independently or with a reading buddy. After children have had many opportunities to read their books in school, send the books home for extra skill-building practice. Encourage children to store the books in a special box that they have labeled "I Can Read Box."

Directions for Making the Instant Books

There are four basic formats for the instant books in this guide. The directions appear below for quick and easy reference. The directions are written *to the child*, in case you would like to send the bookmaking activities home as homework. Just copy the directions and attach them to the instant book pages.

Flip Book, pages 5–6, 7–8, 10–11, 12–13, 15–16, 17–18, 19–20

1. Cut out the flip book and picture cards.
2. Say the name of each picture and listen to the beginning sound.
3. Sort the picture cards and staple them to the correct page.
4. Read your book!

Strip Book, pages 9, 14, 21

1. Say the name of each picture. Write the letter that makes the beginning sound.
2. Cut out the strips.
3. Put the strips in order. Staple them on the left.
4. Read your book!

Optional: Make and decorate a construction paper cover, and color the pictures.

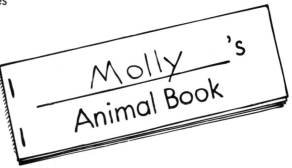

Word Wallet, pages 22–23, 24–25, 26–27, 28–29

1. Trace the dotted letters on the wallet.
2. Cut out the wallet.
3. Fold it in half along the solid middle line.
4. Staple where shown. Tape the outer edges. Fold the wallet closed.
5. Cut out the picture cards. Sort them into the correct pockets.

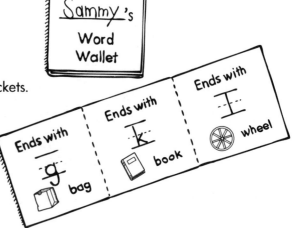

Shape Book, pages 30, 31, 32

1. Write the missing letters on each word card.
2. Cut out the shape and the word cards.
3. Staple the word cards to the shape.
4. Practice reading your words!

Build-a-Skill *Instant Books • Beginning and Ending Consonant Sounds* © 2015 Creative Teaching Press

Flip Book

Begins with **b**

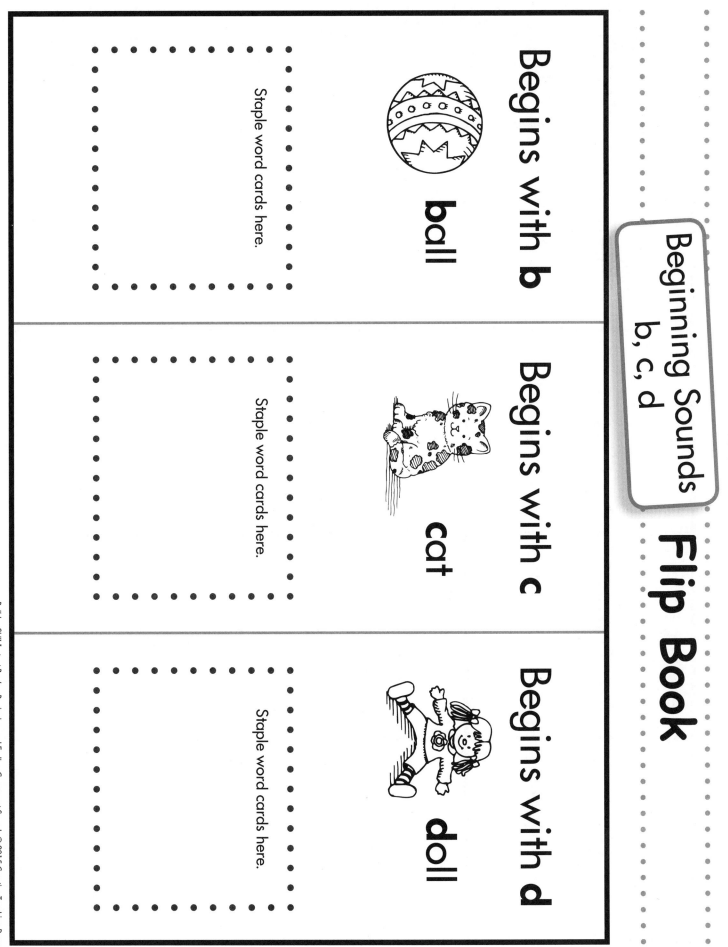

ball

Staple word cards here.

Begins with **c**

cat

Staple word cards here.

Begins with **d**

doll

Staple word cards here.

Beginning Sounds b, c, d

Picture Cards

Build-a-Skill Instant Books • Beginning and Ending Consonant Sounds © 2015 Creative Teaching Press

Flip Book

Begins with f

fan

Staple word cards here.

Begins with g

girl

Staple word cards here.

Begins with h

hat

Staple word cards here.

Build-a-Skill Instant Books • Beginning and Ending Consonant Sounds © 2015 Creative Teaching Press

Brent _____'s
Animal Book

begins with _____

begins with _____

begins with _____

begins with _____

_____'s
Animal Book

begins with _____

begins with _____

begins with _____

Flip Book

**Beginning Sounds
j, k, l**

Begins with l

lamp

Staple word cards here.

Begins with k

kick

Staple word cards here.

Begins with j

jet

Staple word cards here.

Build-a-Skill Instant Books • Beginning and Ending Consonant Sounds © 2015 Creative Teaching Press

Flip Book

Beginning Sounds
m, n, p

Begins with p

pig

Staple word cards here.

Begins with n

nut

Staple word cards here.

Begins with m

mask

Staple word cards here.

Beginning Sounds m, n, p

Picture Cards

My Playtime Strip Book

Hannah's
Playtime Book

_____'s
Playtime Book

_ _ _ _
begins with

_ _ _ _
begins with

_ _ _ _
begins with

_ _ _ _
begins with

_ _ _ _
begins with

_ _ _ _
begins with

_ _ _ _
begins with

Build-a-Skill Instant Books • Beginning and Ending Consonant Sounds © 2015 Creative Teaching Press

Flip Book

Begins with **q**

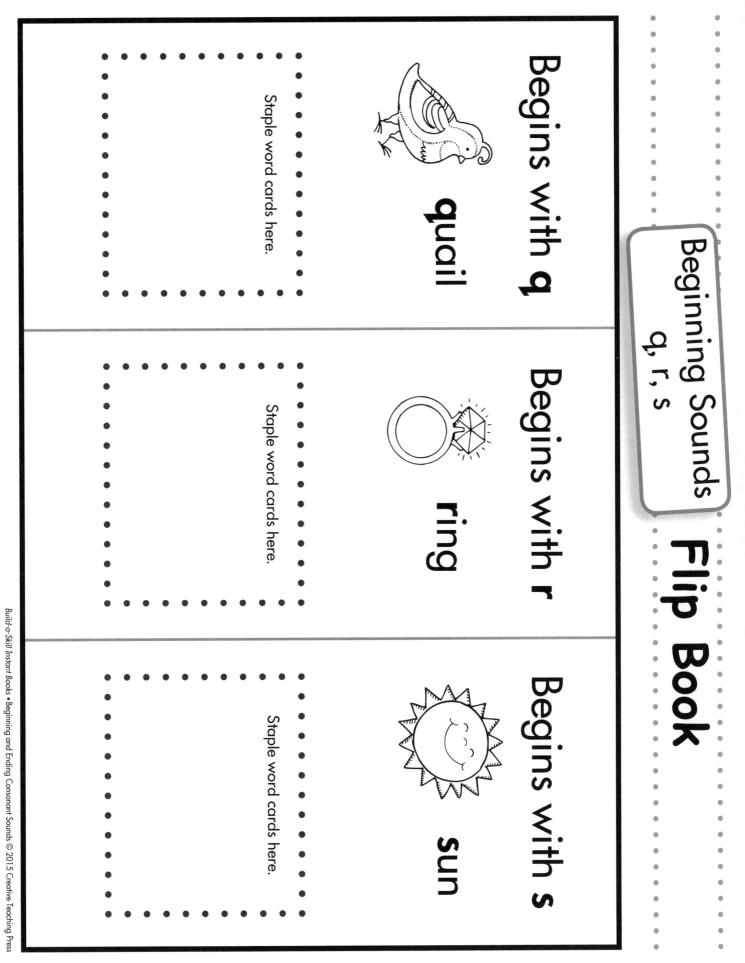

quail

Staple word cards here.

Begins with **r**

ring

Staple word cards here.

Begins with **s**

sun

Staple word cards here.

Build-a-Skill Instant Books • Beginning and Ending Consonant Sounds © 2015 Creative Teaching Press

Build-a-Skill Instant Books • Beginning and Ending Consonant Sounds © 2015 Creative Teaching Press

Flip Book

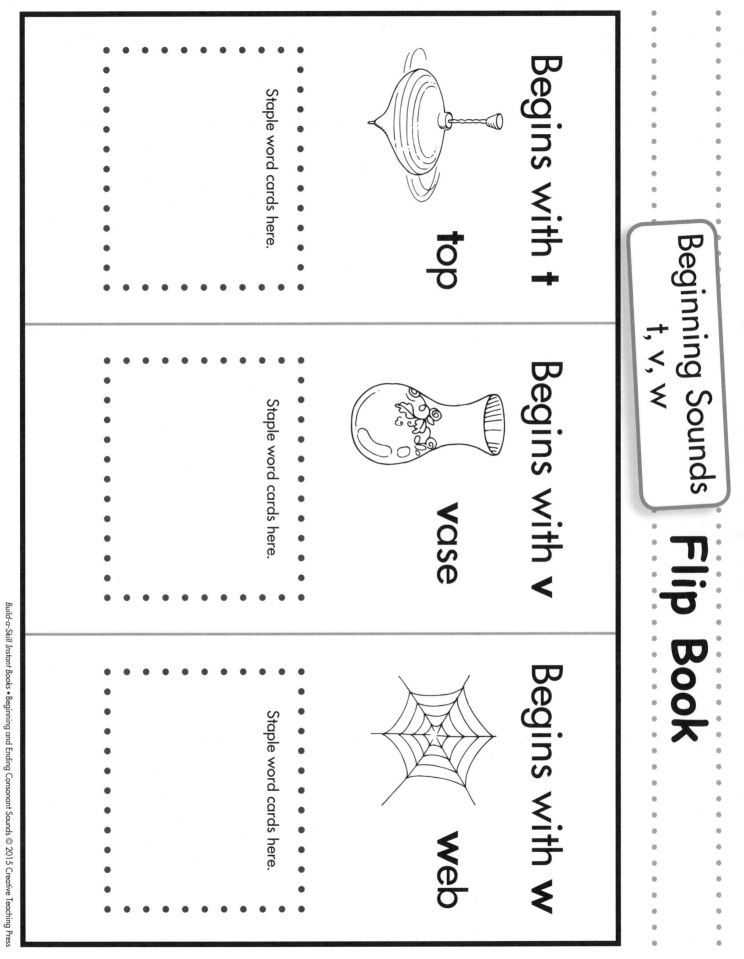

Begins with t

top

Staple word cards here.

Begins with v

vase

Staple word cards here.

Begins with w

web

Staple word cards here.

Picture Cards

Build-a-Skill Instant Books • Beginning and Ending Consonant Sounds © 2015 Creative Teaching Press

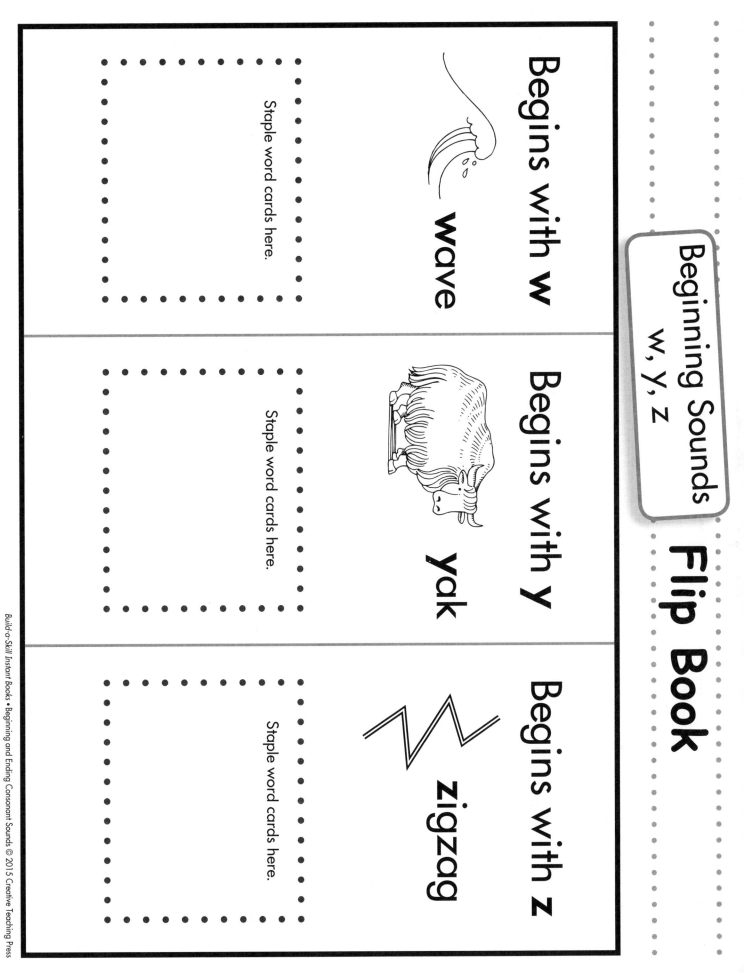

Begins with **w**

wave

Staple word cards here.

Begins with **y**

yak

Staple word cards here.

Begins with **z**

zigzag

Staple word cards here.

Build-a-Skill Instant Books • Beginning and Ending Consonant Sounds © 2015 Creative Teaching Press

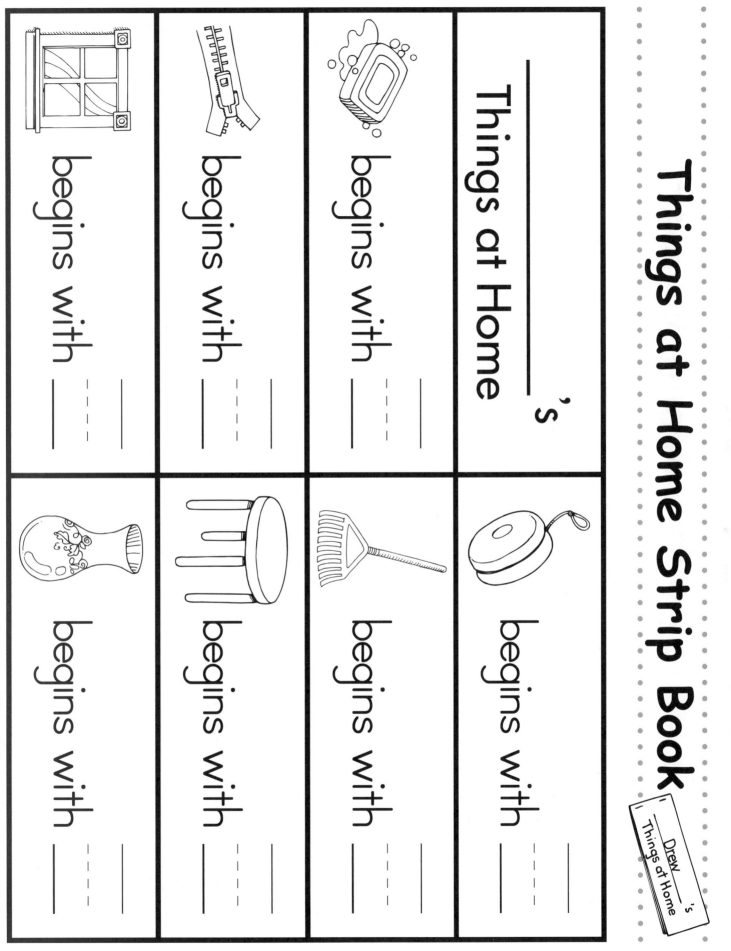

Drew____'s
Things at Home

Things at Home

____'s

begins with ____

begins with ____

begins with ____

begins with ____

begins with ____

begins with ____

begins with ____

Word Wallet

Ending Sounds
b, d, f

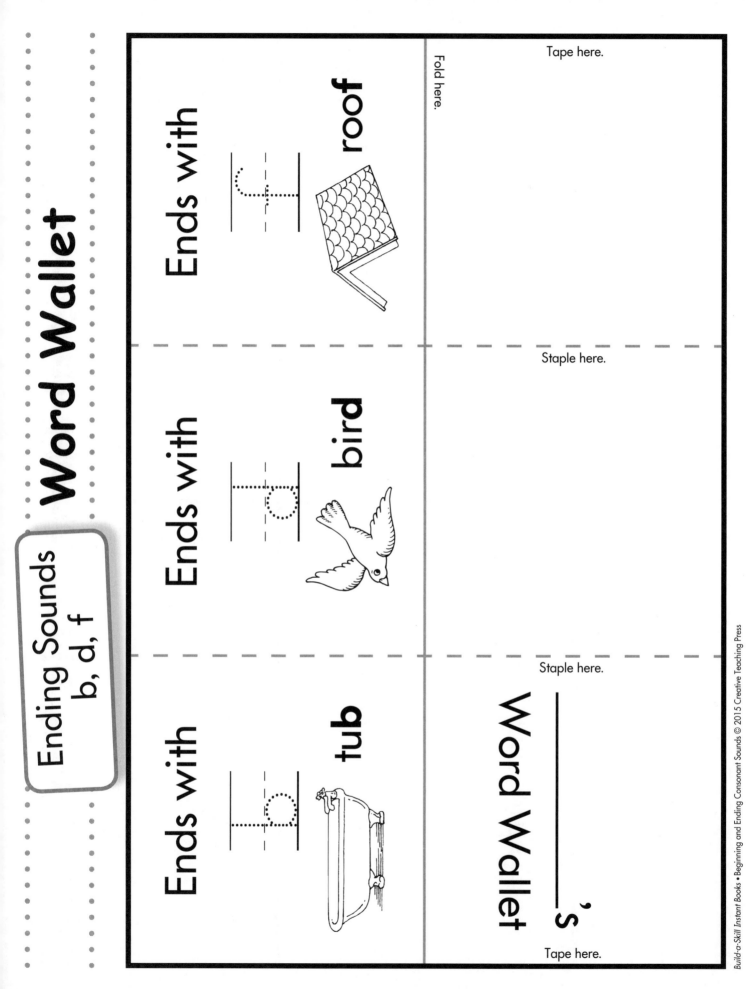

Tape here.

Fold here.

Ends with

roof

Staple here.

Ends with

bird

Staple here.

Ends with

tub

Word Wallet

's

Tape here.

Wallet Pictures

Build-a-Skill Instant Books • Beginning and Ending Consonant Sounds © 2015 Creative Teaching Press

Word Wallet

Ends with

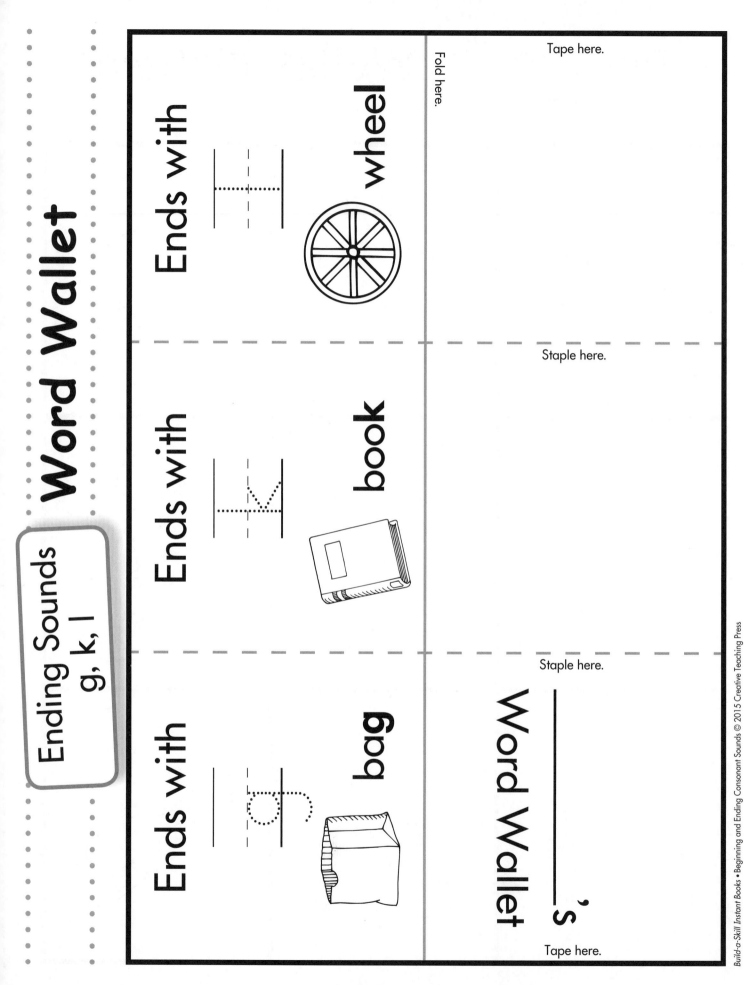

Ends with

wheel

Tape here.

Fold here.

Staple here.

Ends with

book

Staple here.

Word Wallet

's

bag

Tape here.

Build-a-Skill Instant Books • Beginning and Ending Consonant Sounds © 2015 Creative Teaching Press

Wallet Pictures

Word Wallet

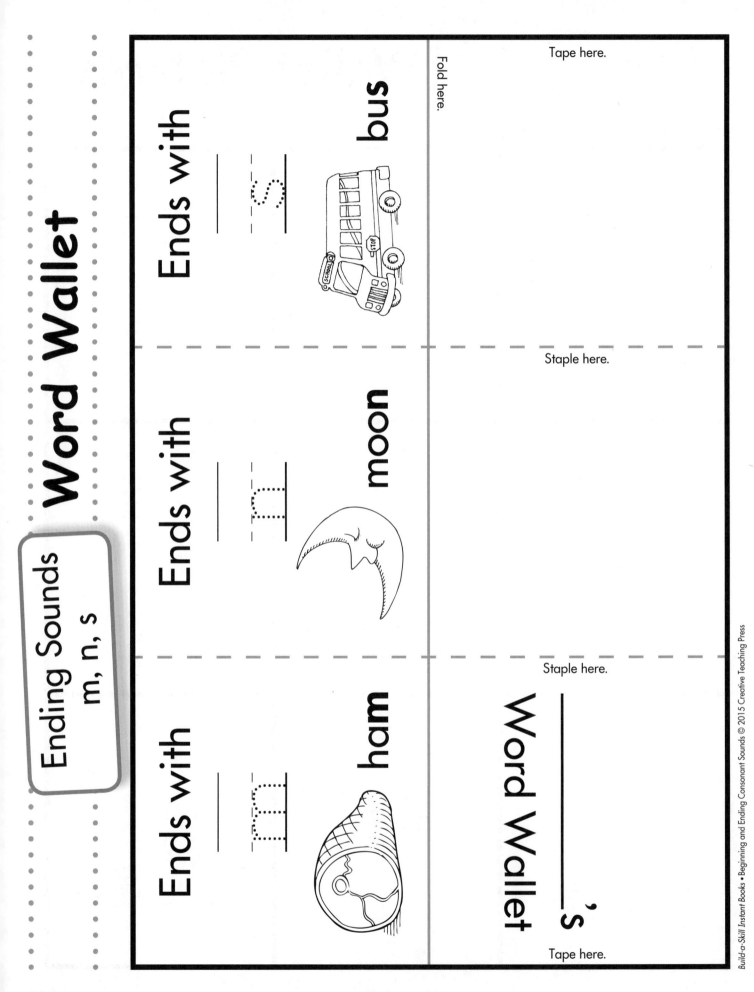

Tape here.

Fold here.

Ends with

___ s

bus

Staple here.

Ends with

___ n

moon

Staple here.

Ends with

___ m

ham

Word Wallet

___'s

Tape here.

Build-a-Skill Instant Books • Beginning and Ending Consonant Sounds © 2015 Creative Teaching Press

Word Wallet

Ending Sounds
p, t, x

Ends with

fox

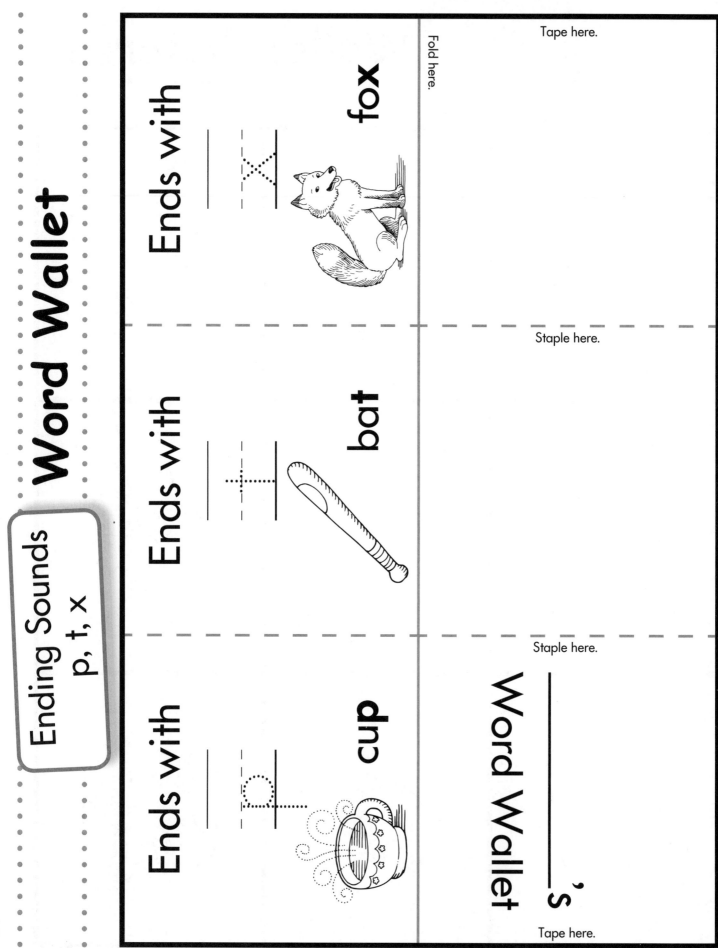

Tape here.

Fold here.

Staple here.

Ends with

bat

Ends with

cup

Word Wallet

's

Word Wallet

Staple here.

Tape here.

Build-a-Skill Instant Books • Beginning and Ending Consonant Sounds © 2015 Creative Teaching Press

Shape Book

Trucking Along

Staple cards here.

_____ u _____

_____ u _____

_____ e _____

_____ o _____

_____ a _____

_____ e _____

Build-a-Skill Instant Books • Beginning and Ending Consonant Sounds © 2015 Creative Teaching Press

Shape Book

Now Hear This!

Staple cards here.

____u____   ____e____

____a____   ____a____

____o____   ____i____

Build-a-Skill Instant Books • Beginning and Ending Consonant Sounds © 2015 Creative Teaching Press

I Know Letters and Sounds

Staple cards here.

__ e __

__ a __

__ o __

__ i __

__ u __

__ o __

Build-a-Skill Instant Books • Beginning and Ending Consonant Sounds © 2015 Creative Teaching Press